John Corbet

A Discourse of the Religion of England

Asserting that reformed Christianity setled in its due latitude, is the

stability and advancement of this kingdom

John Corbet

A Discourse of the Religion of England
Asserting that reformed Christianity setled in its due latitude, is the stability and advancement of this kingdom

ISBN/EAN: 9783337172305

Printed in Europe, USA, Canada, Australia, Japan

Cover: Foto ©Lupo / pixelio.de

More available books at **www.hansebooks.com**

A
DISCOURSE
OF THE
RELIGION
OF
ENGLAND.

ASSERTING,

That REFORMED CHRISTIANITY
setled in its Due Latitude, is the Stability and Advancement of this KINGDOM.

By John Corbett

LONDON, Printed in the Year M. DC. LX. VII.

A

DISCOURSE

OF THE

RELIGION

OF

ENGLAND.

ASSERTING,

That Reformed Christianity
setled in its Due Latitude, is the Stability and Advancement of this Kingdom.

LONDON, Printed in the Year M.DC.LX.VII.

THE
PREFACE.

REligion being deeply imprinted in
Humane Nature, and having a great
Power over it, and being more nota-
bly displayed in the present Age, is become
the Grand Interest of *States*, and almost
of all men, though not after the same manner, nor upon the same Grounds and Mo-
tives. For this cause, whether it comes in
Truth, or in Shew only, it is found to
rule and turn about the great Affairs of
the World. And though many things of
different nature, may have great influence on the State of this Kingdom, yet
Religion and *Matters of Conscience* evi-

dently

evidently appear to have the greateſt. The diſtinguiſhing of Perſons for the favour or disfavour of the Times; yea, the very Names of Diſcrimination paſs upon the account of *Religious Differences.* The Active part of all ſorts and ranks of men, is hereby chiefly ſwayed in their Motions; and their Affections move more importunately in this One, then in all their other Concernments. Wherefore if a Settlement may be found out, which may accommodate all thoſe Parties or Perſwaſions, in which the Peace of the Nation is bound up, it will prove the undoubted Intereſt of this State. And if ſuch a Settlement be likewiſe found to be the true and ſound ſtate of Religion, it muſt needs be acceptable to the faithful Servants of Chriſt, and the true Lovers of their Country.

Now the Adventure of this Diſcourſe is

is to Affert, *That Reformed Chriftianity
rightly ftated, and fetled in its due Latitude,
is the Stability and Advancement of the
Kingdom of* England. Nothing is here
fuggefted for Politick Ends, to corrupt
the Purity, or enervate the Power of Religion, or to leffen Charity; but the Fa-
therly Compaffion of Rulers, and the
mutual Brotherly Condefcention of all
Chriftians, required by the Law of
Chrift, and fome Connivence in cafe of
infuperable Neceffities, and that for the
Truth's fake, is here propounded. *Epi-
fcopacy* is not undermined, nor any other
Form of Government here infinuated;
only a Relaxation of the Prefcribed Uniformity, and fome Indulgence to Diffenters of Sound Faith, and Good Life, is
fubmiffively offered to the Confideration
of our Superiors. All Pragmatical Ar-
rogance, prefuming to give Rules to Go-

vernours, and to teach them what to do,
is carefully avoided; only the Poſſibility,
Expediency, and Neceſſity of Moderation, is repreſented. And it is humbly
deſired, That this Honeſt Intention in
purſuance of Peace, may find a favou-
rable Reception.

The

The Contents.

Sect.

The Contents.

ERRATA.

Page 9. line 2. read *in King James his time.* p.5. l. 18. r. *Arts of Rome.* p.31. l. 31. r. *exacted.*

A

A
DISCOURSE
OF THE
RELIGION of *ENGLAND*.

SECT. I.

*The Religion of this Realm, and three different Parties of
most important consideration; The* Protestants *of the*
Church of England, *the* Protestant Nonconformists, *and
the* Papists.

THE Religion of *England* considered, not only as
established by Law, but as rooted in the Nation,
and generally embraced, is that which is called
Protestant, and is no other then Christianity recovered out of the Antichristian Apostacy, and reformed
from the Corruptions of later Ages, after the Primitive Purity; receiving the holy Scriptures as the perfect Rule of
Christian Faith and Life.

Howbeit, in this Realm there be three different Parties
of most important consideration : The first consists of those
Protestants that zealously adhere to the English Ecclesiastical Polity, and call themselves the *Church of England.* The

second sort is of those Protestants that receive the Doctrine of Faith contained in the Articles of Religion, but are diffatisfied in the form of Ecclefiaftical Polity. These by their Adverfaries have been ufually called *Puritans.* The third is of thofe that utterly reject the Reformation, and remain united to the Pope as their Spiritual Head, and call themfelves *Roman-Catholicks.*

Hereupon an impartial ferious Obferver, refpecting the Common Good, may be induced to make inquiry, How agreeable or dif-harmonious each of thefe Three are to the Publick Weal; as alfo, What proportion they bear to each other; and whether thofe under the Legal Eftablifhment, or the Diffenters, preponderate in the Ballance of the Nation; or whether the Eftablifhed preponderate in that degree which is requifite in true reafon of Government.

SECT. II.

The Behaviour and Pretenfions of the POPISH Party in thefe Times.

THE *Roman-Catholicks* in *England,* confidered not barely in their Number, but in their Rank and Quality, being Rich and Powerful, and Strong in Alliances, are very momentous, and feem to be capable of great Defigns, efpecially in conjunction with Foreign Interefts.

In thefe times they have taken much Liberty and Boldnefs, with an undifturbed Security, and lately have been obferved to be more then ordinarily active, jocund and confident of the effect of their Mutual Correfpondencies; and manifold paffages of dangerous appearance have been every where fpoken of; in fo much that the Nation hath taken an Alarm, and the PARLIAMENT judged the Matter worthy of their Search, and appointed a Committee to receive Informations.
This

This Party hath high pretensions of Merit towards the King, and all that are called *Royallists*; and they seek apparently more then Indulgence and Safety, even High Power and Trust, as if they were the true and sure Confidents of this State. Such Claims as these, challenge a serious Debate. For a Charge of a high nature (as themselves have taken notice) hath been of a long time prosecuted against Popery, viz. *That it disposeth Subjects to Rebellion. That it persecutes all other Religions within its reach. That wheresoever it finds incouragement, it is restless, till it bear down all, or hath put all in Disorder.* Till they make a better Defence then the world hath yet seen, we take the just liberty of insisting upon this Charge, and examining first, How benign or safe the influence of Popery is upon any State or Kingdom whatsoever; and then how it doth comport with the State of *England*, whose Basis is the Protestant Religion, setled by Law, and by length of time generally spred, and deeply rooted in the Nation, and solemnly and constantly avowed by Prince and People.

SECT. III.

That POPERY disposeth Subjects to Rebellion.

WHat hath been the constant practice of the Popes, who are the Head of the *Roman* Faith, the Universal consent of History bears record. What continual thundering of Excommunications hath sounded throughout the Christian world in all Ages, since the beginning of the Papal Reign, against Kings, Emperors, and other Princes and States, that presumed to dispute their Dictates, or cross their Designs, to the loosing of Subjects from the Bonds of Allegiance, and the deposing of Soveraigns? What unexampled Abasements hath the Imperial Majesty suffered in the Persons of sundry Emperors, by prodigious

digious

digious inſtances of Papal Pride ; which, though enough
to ſtir up the indignation of mankind, are applauded by famous Writers, Champions of the Court of *Rome?* The
Popes Temporal Dominions began and grew up in Rebellion and Uſurpation, for which cauſe they have nouriſhed
Factions, and filled the world with Warrs and Tumults, and
maintained moſt outragious and tedious Conflicts with many Emperors, even till they had crippled and broke the
back of the Empire it ſelf.

And theſe practices are juſtified by their Decretals and
Canons, and Divines of greateſt Authority, and ſome of
their Councils, aſcribing to the Pope a Power of Depoſing
Princes that are Heretical, or favourers of Hereticks. The
Jeſuits Doctrine of KING-KILLING, hath made them
odious ; and if ſome paſſages can be alledged out of their
Writings againſt taking away the Lives of Princes, their
declared meaning is, That a King depoſed by the Pope, becomes *Tirannus titulo*, and is no more a Lawful King, and
then what follows, is eaſily underſtood. Thoſe of the
Church of *Rome* that diſavow theſe things, ſhould mind
their contradiction to the Faith they own, in leaving their
Popes, Divines and Canoniſts in a point of ſuch importance. But how potent the influence of the Court of *Rome*,
and the Agency of the Jeſuits is for the diffuſing of thoſe
Principles into the moſt and chiefeſt of the *Roman-Catholicks*, is not unknown.

If the undiſturbed Government of the Emperor, and
of the King of *Spain* in later times, be brought forth as an
inſtance of the Loyalty of Popiſh Subjects, or an argument
of the ſoundneſs of Popiſh Principles ; it muſt be conſi-
dered, That the Houſe of *Auſtria* have made their devotion to the See of *Rome*, their grand and appropriate Intereſt, and that See hath a main dependance on thoſe Princes ; and both it and they have the ſame active Votaries

through-

throughout Christendom, the Jesuits and their Adherents.
As for the Kingdom of *France*, the State of *Venice*, and
others acknowledging the Popes Headship, they have had
enough to do, and they would have more, if either themselves were weak, and less formidable to the Pope, or the
Popes lightning and thunder were now as dreadful as in former Ages. Even in Popish Countreys the abuses of Papal
Power, and the Intrigues and Interests of the Court of
Rome are a little better discerned; therefore those Princes
and States can make the better terms for themselves; yet if
either the former degree of ignorance and stupid devotion
to that See, shall return upon their people, or the like oc-
casions of embroiling or breaking States, shall revive, they
must accept the Popes conditions, and submit to the former
yoke.

But if the Princes of that Profession can in this our more
knowing Age, with much ado hold their Subjects in obedience, against the Acts of *Rome*; yet the question concerning *England* remains intire, Whether a Protestant Prince
can with good reason confide or repose himself in the Loyalty of his Popish Subjects? and more especially, Whether the fore-mentioned Popish Claims do in any wise
comport with the State of *England*, whose Basis is the Protestant Religion?

No other Religion gives the Priests such an Empire over
the Conscience, as the Popish doth. The Principles of
that Belief, and the Order and Frame of that Church, are
directed to this end, and the people are miserably inthral-
led to the will of their Clergy: By Auricular Confession
the Priests have a constant inlet into the hearts of men, by
injoyning Penances and works of Devotion, they exercise
a spiritual Dominion over them. Hereby they have dayly
opportunity, and advantage enough to excite them to any
notable Exploits for the Catholick Cause; unto which kind
of

of services they fix an Opinion of the highest Merit, either for discharge from the pains of Purgatory, or for the acquest of a greater Reward in Glory: Yea, dissolute persons may be easily drawn to such Attempts, in hope of making compensation for a loose and lewd life; and when they suffer for Sedition or Treason, they are held to acquire the glory of Martyrs and Confessors. Add hereunto their Belluine hatred of Hereticks, and vile esteem of their persons: And in all this, their Church's supposed Infallibility warrants this blind obedience, and brutish confidence. And to make void all the security that can be given between Prince and people, the Pope under pretence of Equity and Necessity, undertakes to dispence with Oaths, and with all Laws both Civil and Divine. Besides all this, there is the Jesuits peculiar Discipline, most exquisite for blind obedience and resolution, and consequently, for any great and strange Attempts.

Things past may afford prognosticks of thing to come. May *Englands* constant Experience be taken for Evidence in the case*. The Reign of Queen *Elizabeth*, after the Protestant Reformation had gotten the stated possession of this Kingdom, was infested with a continued succession and series of Treasons, for the re-introducing of Popery, carried on by the English Papists with an indefatigable and implacable Spirit, proceeding from Causes peculiar to that Religion.

*In the Reign of Edward the sixth, a formidable Rebellion was raised for the recovery of the Mass.

During the first ten years, they conformed to the Church of *England*; but afterwards, to testifie their union with the Pope, they became a divided party in this State. For then the Queen being found unmoveable, the Pope published his Declaratory Sentence against Her, by which all Her Subjects were absolved from the Oath of Allengiance, and

an

an *Anathema* denounced against those that thenceforth obey Her. The Popish Rebellion in the North breaks out. Many horrid attempts of Violence upon Her Majesties Person, were plotted one after another for many years together, as that of Dr. *Story*, of *Parry*, of *Arden* and *Somervile*, of *Throgmorton*, of *Babington* and his Complices, besides the concurrent Commotion in *Ireland* *. In these several Treasons, many of the Seminary Priests were forward and active. The great and setled Design, was the advancing of the Queen of *Scots*, to the Crown of *England*; wherein were ingaged the Pope, and *Spaniard*, and *French* King, and Duke of *Guise*, in conjunction with the *English Papists*, making use of her Title to set on foot those many desperate Enterprises against the Queen.

* Dr. *Parry* confessed that having promised at *Rome* to kill the Queen, he was troubled in Conscience about it, till he had read Dr. *Allen*'s Book, which taught, That Princes excommunicate for Heresie, were to be deprived of Kingdom and Life; which Book, he said, did vehemently excite him to prosecute his Enterprise.

After the death of the Queen of *Scots*, they raised a new Title to the Crown in the House of *Spain*. The memory of Eighty Eight, will be an everlasting Monument of Papistical Cruelty and Treason. Cardinal *Allen* the first founder or procurer of the Foreign Seminaries, a person admired as well by the Secular Priests, as Jesuits, penned a Treatise with all the Rhetorick he had, to excite the *English* Catholicks to joyn with the *Spaniards*. Among the Forces in the *Low-Countries* prepared for this Invasion, were seven hundred *English* Fugitives. After the *Spanish* Armado was dissipated, the Jesuits had not done. They would have stirred up the Earl of *Derby* to assume the Title of the Kingdom; they plotted the poysoning of the Queen by *Lopez* her Physician; they excited Villains to dispatch her by bloody hands, and they never left soliciting the King of *Spain*, till he twice attempted another Invasion. In those times

times *Parsons* his Book of Titles was famous, wherein he set up divers Competitors for the Crown, preferring the Infanta before all others, and slighting King *James* his Title, as having but few Favourers, and little accounted by Catholicks.

The *Roman* party could be provoked to these mischiefs by no other impulse then the impetuous zeal of their Superstition. Some of their own did then publish to the world their important Considerations, to move all true Catholicks to acknowledg, That the proceedings of Her Majesty and the State, with them, since the beginning of Her Reign, had been mild and merciful. In the several times of those mischievous designments, though some priests were executed, yet those that were found moderate in their Examinations, obtained Mercy, and a great number of them that by Law were obnoxious to death, were spared from that extremity, and only banished. It is true, that certain Secular priests did impute all those Treasons to the Jesuits and their Adherents, and fully charged them with all the aforesaid matters of Fact, in terms of highest aggravation, acquitting all other Catholicks. But it must be noted, that the Jesuits were in greatest reputation, and had the predominant influence upon the *English Papists* in general, and (as appears by the Seculars loud Complaints) had such a power of disposing the Alms collected for their prisoners, and other sufferers, that such as complied not with their purposes, were debarr'd of relief, and pined for want. And by their counsels, the Foreign Seminaries, those Nurseries of Disloyalty were wholly swayed. And 'tis observable, That the agrieved Seculars never published their pretended abhorrency of these Treasons, till they were over-past, and themselves, being driven to despair by the Jesuits potency, were forced to take shelter under a great Prelate of the Church of *England*.

The

The same Spirit of Disloyalty was as active and vigorous in that Kings time, who at his first entrance, found himself excluded from Title to the Crown, by two Papal Breves, the ground-work of that Infernal Plot of matchless Villany and Cruelty, the *GUNPOWDER-TREASON*. After the defeat of which horrid Conspiracy, the Projects of *Rome* proceeded not in such down-right Rebellions, which always miscarried; but in ways more secretly undermining Religion, and as truly destructive to the Interest of King and Kingdom.

SECT. IV.

That it Persecutes all other Religions within its reach.

THE second Branch of the Charge against *Popery*, is, *That it persecutes all other Religions within its reach.* In the Church of *Rome*, for many by-past Ages, the Meekness of Christ, and the Dove-like nature of his Spouse hath not appeared, but the Cruelty of that great Whore that was drunken with the Blood of the Saints, and of the Martyrs of Jesus. All that cast off her yoke, and disown her pretended Infallibility, are with her no better then Hereticks, though they intirely own all the Articles of the Christian Faith received by the ancient Church. And Hereticks are esteemed more vile then dogs; and it is held meritorious to abuse and torment them. Her Laws have made their punishment to be the sharpest kind of death, Burning alive inexorably inflicted. By this *Romish* Wrath and Fury were Three hundred Martyrs sacrificed in Queen *Maries* time, for not believing the Sacramental Bread to be turned into the Substance of Chrifts Body, against the most clear and distinct perception and reason of all Mankind.

But can humane Nature hear, without horror, the report of that direful Consistory, called the *Holy Inquisition*, esta-

C   blish-

blished in those Countries where *Popery* is in full sway. Doubtless that Church whose Religious Orders in a solemn and Sacred Judicatory, shall commit such horrid Outrages as are indeed acted by those Infernal Judges, upon pretence of Justice and Piety, must needs be a School of Universal Cruelty for all her Adherents.

The *Popish* hath outgone the *Pagan Cruelty*. What Treachery and Villany hath been acted! What barbarous Indignities have been offered in ways as immodest and shameless, as outragious and merciless, upon pretence of zeal against Hereticks! What varieties of strangely-devised Torments have been inflicted upon the Servants of Christ, without sparing Age, Sex, or Condition! Nor hath such work been done onely in our Age or Country, but in all Ages successively, and Countries universally, that were imbued with *Romish* Principles: Witness the huge slaughters of the *Waldenses*, the persecutions of the *Bohemian* Brethren, and of many others throughout Christendom in the former Ages: And since *Protestant-Reformation*, how have the *Romish Zealots* filled *Europe* with the slaughters of Christians within their reach, in *France*, *Germany*, *Spain*, *Italy*, *England*, *Scotland*, the *Netherlands*. In *Ireland*, *Piedmont* and *Poland*, their Cruelty is fresh in memory. And the slain cannot be numbred for multitude; they were killed by Thousands, Ten thousands, Hundred thousands, at one and the same Persecution. And the Tragedies have been acted where the Name of *Protestant* was well known, yea, where Protestants were under the shelter of the Law. For the Jesuits uncessantly stir up the Princes to fall upon their people against Law, and without provocation given, and after things have been setled, to break their Agreements with them. And the Pope himself is the Contriver or Applauder of these Mischiefs, and the successful execution thereof, is received at *Rome* with joy and triumph, as the Mur-

therers

therers in the *Parisian* Massacre were highly extolled by the Pope, and rewarded with such spiritual Graces as his Holiness useth to bestow.

SECT. V.

That wheresoever it finds Encouragement, it is restless, till it bears down all before it, or hath put all in disorder.

MAy we judg by these things, how a Party devoted to the See of *Rome*, are to be trusted and cherished in a Protestant Nation, who mind the securing of themselves and their posterity, from the sharpest Persecutions; especially considering the Third Branch of the Charge, *That in any State, where they find advantage, or fit matter to work upon, they are restless, till they bear down all, or put all in disorder.*

Popery hath its formed Combinations, and setled Correspondencies over all Christendom, under the Supreme Direction and Government of the Congregation at *Rome*, for the propagation of the Faith; which sent over swarms of *Seminary Priests, Jesuits*, and *Fryars* of all sorts, who made their Hives in *England*.

The several PARLIAMENTS of the later times of King *James*, represented to the King how the *Popish Recusants* had dangerously increased their Numbers and Insolencies, having great expectation from the *Treaties* with *Spain*, and the interposing of *Foreign Princes* for Indulgence to them; how they openly and usually resorted to the Churches and Chappels of *Foreign Ambassadors*, their more then usual concourse to the City, and their frequent Conventicles and Conferences there; how their children were educated in many Foreign *Seminaries* appropriated to the *English* Fugitives; what swarms of Priests and Jesuits came into the Land; many Popish and Seditious Books licentiously

C 2   print-

printed and difperfed. From which Caufes, as from bitter
Roots, moft dangerous Effects both to Church and State
would follow. For the Popifh Religion is incompatible
with ours ; it draws with it an unavoidable dependance upon Foreign Princes ; it opens a wide gap for popularity in
any who fhall draw too great a party ; it hath a reftlefs fpi-
rit, and will ftrive by thefe gradations. If it once get con-
nivance, it will prefs for Toleration ; if that fhould be
obtained, it muft have an Equality ; from thence it will
afpire to a Superiority, and never reft till it hath wrought
the fubverfion of true Religion.

In the feveral *PARLIAMENTS* of King *Charles* the Firft,
not one *Publick Grievance* was more infifted on, then the
Growth of POPERY. In the Third PARLIAMENT
of that King, at a Conference between the Lords and
Commons about *Popifh Recufants*, one of the Principal
Secretaries of State fpake thus: "Give me leave to tell
"you what I know, That Thefe now both vaunt at home,
"and write to their Friends abroad, they hope all will
"be well, and doubt not to prevail, and win ground upon
"us: And a little to awaken the Care and Zeal of our
"Learned and Grave Fathers, it is fit that they take notice
"of that Hierarchy, which is already Eftablifhed in com-
"petition with their Lordfhips: For they have already a
"Bifhop confecrated by the Pope. This Bifhop hath his
"fubalternate Officers of all kinds; as *Vicars General,*
"*Arch-Deacons, Rural Deans, Apparitors*, and fuch like;
"neither are thefe nominal and titular Officers alone, but
"they all execute their Jurifdiction, and make their ordina-
"ry Vifitation throughout the Kingdom, keep Courts, and
"determine Ecclefiaftical Caufes; and, which is an argu-
"ment of more confequence, they keep ordinary intelli-
"gence by their Agents at *Rome*, and hold correfpondencies
"with the Nuncio's and Cardinals both at *Bruxels*, and in
France.

"*France*. Neither are the Seculars alone grown to this
"height, but the Regulars are more active and dangerous,
"and have taken deep root. They have already planted
"their Societies and Colledges of both Sexes. They have
"setled Revenues, Houses, Libraries, Vestments, and all
"other necessary provisions to travel, or stay at home; nay,
"even at this time they intend to hold a concurrent Assem-
"bly with this Parliament.

In *Ireland* a *Popish Clergy* far more numerous then the *Pro-*
testant, was in full exercise of all *Ecclesiastical Jurisdiction*,
by *Arch-Bishops*, *Bishops*, *Vicars*, *General Officiats*, and a *Vicar*
Apostolical. And they had a special *Cardinal* at *Rome* for
their Protector.

Among other Projects, a Consultation and Overture of
reconciling *England* and *Rome*, was set on foot. Some of E-
minency in the Church of *England*, gave advantage to the
Project, by declaring, That only the *Puritans* among the
Protestants, and the *Jesuits* among the *Papists*, obstructed
the Peace of *Christendom*. Some prime Agent of the Pope,
made a solemn offer of a Cardinalship to Bishop *Laud*, at
the time of his translation to the See of *Canterbury*. *San-*
ta Clara presumed to dedicate his Book to the King, wherein the *Articles* of the Church of *England* were examined
by the *Roman Standard*, and distorted to the sense of the
Council of *Trent*. The Pope had Three Nuncio's, *Panza-*
ni, Con, and *Roseti*, successively residing in *England*, to work
upon this State by advantage of the Project of *Reconci-*
liation.

This Faction had many Irons in the Fire, and many strings
to their Bow. They had their Agents in Court, City and
Country. They had their Spyes in the Houses of great
men, and such as kept continual watch over them that had
the chief sway of Publick Affairs. Their work was to
raise and foster Jealousies between the King and His People,

ple, to caſt things into the hurry of Faction, Prejudice and
confuſed Motion. And whether the Court or Popular Faction prevailed, they thought it equally advantagious to
their Deſigns, which was to unſettle the preſent State, and
work Mutations. Such *Incendiaries* are the *Factors* of *Rome*,
and ſuch buſie *Engineers* in the Confuſions of *Chriſtendom*.
Can any that conſiders the foregoing paſſages, doubt of the
powerful and ſpecial Agency of the Court of *Rome*, in
the Commotions that followed. A *Venetian* Agent in *England*, intimate with Nuncio *Panzani*, and privy to all his
Negotiations, made this Obſervation; *If one may make
judgment of things future, by things paſt, this Realm ſo divided into many Factions in matter of Religion, and that of
the Catholick increaſing daily, will in time be troubled and
torn with Civil Warrs.*

SECT. VI.

*The PAPISTS pretenſion of Loyalty and Merit in the King's
Cauſe, Examined.*

THE great Plea and boaſting of the *Romaniſts*, is,
Their pretenſion of Merit in the King's Cauſe. The
truth is, the *Papiſts* knew that the PARLIAMENT was
fully bent, and deeply engaged againſt them, and therefore deſpaired of any good to themſelves by a direct and
open compliance with them, whatever undiſcerned influence they might have on their Counſels: So that Neceſſity made them to ſerve the King in that Warr. And they
brought neither Succeſs nor Reputation to His Majeſties
Affairs; nor did He care to own their Aſſiſtance more then
as juſtified by the preſent neceſſity. And they have little
reaſon to upbraid the *Proteſtants* with the ſcandal of that
Warr; for whatſoever was alledged in defence thereof,
by the PARLIAMENT and their Adherents, as much
hath

hath been written by very Eminent School-men and Doctors of the *Roman* Church, for the Interest of the people, and the Confent of the Cities and the Peers in Defenfive Arms. Which they have written over and above their peculiar Principle of the Popes Univerfal Power of Depofing Kings that are unfit for Government.

As for the woful Cataftrophe of thofe Commotions, it hath been manifefted to the world by fuch as undertook to juftifie it, when Authority fhould require: *That the year before the Kings death, a felect number of Jefuits being fent from their whole Party in* England, *confulted both the Faculty of* Sorbon, *and the* Conclave *at* Rome, *touching the Lawfulnefs and Expediency of promoting the* Change of Government, *by making away the King, whom they defpaired to turn from his Herefie: It was debated and concluded in both places, That for the Advancement of the Catholick Caufe, it was Lawful and Expedient to carry on that Alteration of State.* This Determination was effectually purfued by many Jefuits that came over, and acted their parts in feveral Difguifes. After that execrable Fact was perpetrated on the Perfon of our Soveraign, if we may believe moft credible reports, there were many Witneffes of the great joy among the *Englifh Convents* and *Seminaries*, and other companies of Papifts beyond Sea, as having overcome their great Enemy, and done their main work.

Many of their Chief ones fought the favour of the Ufurpers, with offers of doing them fervice. One of great note among them, in a Book entituled, *Grounds of Obedience and Government*, undertook the folution of the Grand Cafe of thofe Times: *That if a People be diffolved into the ftate of* Anarchy, *their Promife made to their expelled Governour, binds no more; they are remitted to the force of Nature to provide for themfelves. That the old Magiftrates* giſtrates Right, ſtaveis upon the Common Peace, and that is transferred to his Rival, by the Title of Quiet Poſſeſſion. Conformably to theſe Principles, they addreſs their Petition, To the Supream Authority, the PARLIAMENT of the Commonwealth of England. They affirmed, They had generally taken, and punctually kept the Engagement; and promiſed, That if they might enjoy their Religion, they would be the moſt quiet and uſeful Subjects.

Of their Actings ſince His Majeſties Reſtauration, and the Jealouſies and Rumours about them, let men judg as they find by the Evidences that are given.

SECT. VII.

The Reſult of the whole Diſcourſe touching the Popiſh Party.

AND now let it be duly weighed, Whether the Papiſts of theſe Dominions have in later times changed their former Principles and Intereſts, or have only taken another method of greater Artifice and Subtilty, as the change of times hath given them direction and advantage. The ſcope of the whole preceding Diſcourſe, is to call in queſtion thoſe high pretentions of theirs, and to croſs their Aims at great Power and Truſt: But it is not directed againſt the Security of their Perſons or Fortunes, or any meet Indulgence or Clemency towards them. Let them have their Faith to themſelves, without being vexed with ſnares, or any afflicted; the State always providing to obviate the forementioned Principles and Practices of Diſloyalty, and the diffuſing of the leaven of their Superſtition. The Inference of the whole is this, That they be not admitted to a capacity of evil and dangerous influence upon the Affairs of the Kingdom, or of interrupting and perplexing the courſe of things that concern the publike.

SECT.

SECT. VIII.

That the Reformed Religion makes good Christians, and good Subjects.

A S true Religion is the moſt Noble End, ſo it is the beſt Foundation of all Political Government. And it is the felicity of the State of *England*, to reſt upon this Baſis, even Reformed Chriſtianity, or the Primitive and Apoſtolick Religion recovered out of the Apoſtacy of the later times, and ſevered from that new kind of *Paganiſm*, or *Pagano-Chriſtianiſm*, under which it lay much oppreſſed and overwhelmed, but not extinguiſhed. Its wholſome Doctrine contained in its publick Confeſſions, makes *good Chriſtians*, and *good Subjects*. It teacheth obedience to Civil Magiſtrates, without the controle of any Superior or Collateral Power. Nor is it concerned, if dangerous Poſitions fall from the Pens of ſome Writers. And notwithſtanding the Adverſaries Cavils, the Divines of Authority and ſolid Reputation in the Proteſtant Churches, do with a general Conſent maintain the Rights of Princes and Soveraign Powers, againſt all Diſobedience. If any aberration in Practice, hath been found in its Profeſſors, it is not to be charged therewith, becauſe it condemns it ; but the general practice in this point, hath been conformable to the Doctrine.

The Reformation in *England*, for its Legality and Orderlineſs, is unqueſtionable. In *Germany* it was ſetled and defended by Princes and free Cities, that governed their own Signiories and Territories, paying only a reſpect of Homage to the Emperor. In *Helvetia* it began by the Senates of the *Cantons*. It was received in *Geneva* by that Republick, after the Civil Government had been reformed by ſtrong Papiſts. In the Provinces of the *Netherlands* it

was

was spread many years before the Union against the *Spaniard*; which Union was not made upon the score of *Religion*, but of *State*. The manner of its beginning in *Scotland*, is by some attributed to a National Disposition, the asperity and vehemency thereof, is said to be greater in times of *Popery*, and to be much mitigated by the *Reformation*. For *France*, we may take the Testimony of King *JAMES*, who was jealous enough for the Power of Kings. He said, That *he never knew yet, that the* French Protestants *took Arms against their King*. In the first Troubles, they stood only upon their Defence; before they took Arms, they were burned and Massacred every where. The first Quarrel did not begin for Religion, but because when King *Francis* the Second was under Age, they had been the refuge of the Princes of the Blood expelled from the Court, who knew not else where to take Sanctuary; and that it shall not be found that they made any other Warr.

It is not for this Discourse to intermeddle with all the Actions of Protestant Subjects towards their Princes, that have happened in Christendom: Let them stand or fall by the Laws and Polity under which they live. Whensoever they have been disloyal, they have swerved from the known and received Rules of their Profession. Through the corruption of Mankind, Subjects of whatsoever persuasion, are prone to Murmurings and Mutinies. Sometimes Oppression makes them mad. Sometimes a Jealousie of Incroachments upon their Legal Rights and Liberties, raiseth Distempers and Contests. And sometimes an unbridled, wanton affecting of inordinate Liberty, makes them insolent and licentious. But over and above these common Sources of Rebellion, Popery hath a peculiar one, and that of the greatest Force, the Conscience of Religious Obligations, and the Zeal of the Catholick Faith. Protestants have never disowned their King for dif-

ference

ference in Religion, as the most of the *Roman Catholicks* of *France* dealt with *Henry* the Fourth, by the Popes instigation. And in their greatest Enormities, they have never attempted the Stabbing and Poysoning of Princes that stood in their way, which the Jesuits teach their Disciples.

SECT. IX.

The Reformed Religion is the permanent Interest of this Kingdom.

AS the Protestant or Reformed Religion, is the true Primitive Christianity, so it is the stable and permanent Interest of *England*, and the sure Foundation of its Prosperity. The King of *England* is the most Mighty Prince of this Profession, and becomes the more Potent over Christendom, by being the Head and Chief of the whole Protestant Party. And it is well known, That by the Support and Defence of this Cause, the Nation hath encreased in Honour, and Wealth, and Power.

The Peoples rooted Aversness from Popery, is most apparent, and their Jealousies work upon any more then usual Insolence or Confidence of the Papists. The *Royallists* as well as others, have been Allarm'd, and manifested their Zeal against it. And His Majesties Aversness from it, is so fully declared by His Constancy amidst Temptations, in the time of His Exile, and now since His Return, that for His Honours sake, it is made very penal for any to suggest that He would introduce it ; the Law presuming, That such suggestion must needs proceed from an evil mind.

And what Prince that hath cast off the *Popes* yoke, would willingly come under it again ? A Foreign Statesman of the *Roman* Profession, hath observed it as a Barr

D 2   against

against the projected Reconciliation between *England* and *Rome*, That it could not be effected without Concessions on both sides, contrary to the Maxims of both parties. *This Realm* (saith he) *is perversly addicted to maintain its own resolute Opinion of Excluding the Popes Authority. And the Court of* Rome *is more sollicitous to remove whatsoever is contrary to its Temporal Grandure, then to extirpate such Heresies as this Realm is infected with.* To instance in that one point of the Approbation or Toleration of the Oath of Allegiance; though some Catholick Doctors had with their Tongues and Pens maintained the lawfulness of that Oath; yet thereby, and by opening some other points of high consequence, they had so displeased the Pope, that could they have been catch't, they were sure to have been burn'd or strangled for it. But what allurement is there to dispose the Monarchs of the Earth to subject themselves to the Sacerdotal Empire of *Rome*, or to endeavour an Accommodation with it? Hath Popery its advantages to dispose Subjects to security and blind obedience? So it hath its advantages to loosen the Bonds of Allegiance, and foment Rebellion in Subjects; when Protestancy seasons them with principles of unstained Loyalty. A people nuzled in ignorance and superstition, are more easily seduced from their obedience to Magistrates, and carried headlong by those that have dominion over their Consciences. But Understanding and Knowledg makes men considerate, and more easily manageable by a just and prudent Government.

As for the Clergy's Interest, though the Protestant Religion doth not affect that excessive Pomp and Splendor of Church-men, which the Popish doth; yet it is taken for granted, That neither Conscience nor Interest will permit the Bishops and Clergy of *England*, to unite to the See of *Rome.* Their Doctrine is too pure, and their Judgment too

clear

clear for a full compliance with Popery: And they know what it is to come under the Papal Yoke, to divest themselves, and receive new Orders from *Rome*, and to be displaced and set behind the *Veteran* Soldiers of the *Roman* Camp, whose turns must be first served.

SECT. X.

It is for the behoof of Religion and true Piety, and for the Interest of this State, That Reformed Christianity be setled in its full Extent.

IF it be resolved, *That Protestancy is the truth of Christianity*, and also, *the stability of England*; it follows, That this Profession must not be streightned and lessened, but inlarged and cherished, according to its true Extent; and the Rule and Square of the Ecclesiastical State, must be commensurate thereunto. It should be the measure of all mens Zeal and Activity in Rites and Opinions, whatsoever is necessary to its support and advancement, is constantly to be asserted; and about things impertinent thereunto, contention should utterly cease. This is to advance the Kingdom of God among men, and to encrease the Church's glory upon earth. But by needless Schisms and Factions, to weaken the common Interest of Reformed Christianity, is to dissipate the Church of God, and to defeat the great Ends of the Christian Religion, which are, Sound and strong Faith in Christ and his Promises, unfeigned devotion, purity of heart, innocence and integrity of life, common charity, brotherly love, humility, mutual forbearance, and condescention, unshaken peace and concord.

As this Latitude promotes the great Designs of Christs Gospel, so it settles this Nation, and is, for matter of Religion, its right and sure Basis. Every good Foundation, lyes adequate to the Building to be laid thereon: So any Polity
Civil

Civil or Ecclefiaftical, fhould be proportionate to the people to be governed thereby.   The people that are of moment in the Ballance of this Nation, are, though not uni-
verfally, yet more generally rooted in *Proteftantifm*, as it is
taken in its due latitude, and not as unduly reftrained by the
paffions and interefts of men : For in this they are one,
though divided about leffer things.

There hath been much difcord between men of feveral
Perfwafions, that throughly accord with each other in the
fame common Faith, as almoft to expunge one another
out of the Lift of *Proteftants*. Surely this is a great error
and a difadvantage on all hands, as well to thofe that ftand
on the Vantage-ground, as to others : For they that carry
it after this fort, do weaken the Common Intereft of true
Religion, and ftrengthen the Common Adverfary that is
irreconcilable, and difparage themfelves as a narrow Party
or Faction.   That all thofe who heartily embrace the *Englifh Reformation* eftablifhed by Law, are Proteftants, will
not be queftioned by men of temperate fpirits. And
concerning the refidue, let the fober-minded judge, Whether they that affent to the Doctrine of Faith contained
in the Articles of the *Church of England*, and do worfhip
God according to that Faith, have right to be efteemed
Proteftants. Now if Proteftancy taken in its due Extent, doth fway the Nation, and is able to fettle its Peace
againft the Competition of any *Rival*; fhould it not be en-
compaffed according to that Extent, as much as is poffible,
in the Polity of this State?

SECT. XI.

How momentous in the Ballance of the Nation, those Prote-
stants are, that dissent from the present Ecclesiastical
Polity.

VVHether cogent Reason speaks for this Latitude,
be it now considered, *How momentous in the*
Ballance of this Nation, those Protestants are, which are dis-
satisfied in the present Ecclesiastical Polity. They are every
where spred through City and Countrey; they make no
small part of all ranks and sorts of men; by Relations and
Commerce they are so woven into the Nations Interest,
that it is not easie to sever them, without unravelling the
whole. They are not excluded from among the *Nobility,*
among the *Gentry* they are not a few; but none are of more
importance then they in the Trading part of the people,
and those that live by Industry, upon whose hands the Business of the Nation lyes much. It hath been noted, that
some who bear them no good will, have said, *That the very*
Air of Corporations is infected with their Contagion. And in
whatsoever degree they are, high or low, ordinarily for
good understanding, steddiness and soberness, they are
not inferior to others of the same Rank and Quality; neither do they want the Rational Courage of *English*
Men.

As for the Ministers of this Perswasion, some have called them *Fools* for their *Inconformity*; others are reported to have said, *That the Church should not so easily be rid*
of them, as if their Conformity had been dreaded by them.
Some have pitied them, wishing *that they would Conform;*
and others revile them, saying, *Conform, or not Conform,*
never trust them. Howbeit, they make Solemn Appeals
to the Most High God, *That they dare not Conform, for*
Con-

Conscience sake; and *that it is not in the power of their own wills to relieve them*. And whatsoever their grounds of dissent be, they hold it out against all hopes of Indulgence, whilst many of them live in Necessities, and most of them upon the kindness of others.

It is now about Five years since a Full and Vigorous *Act of Uniformity*. at once cleared the Church of the supposed Enemies of her Polity. All Corporations have been New-model'd and changed as to the Principles and Tempers of persons, for the better securing of the Government in Church and State. The Private Meetings for Religious Worship (termed *Conventicles*) are strictly prohibited, Deportation being the Penalty upon the Third Conviction. And for the breaking and dissipating of the whole Party, it is provided by another Law, *That the Non-conforming Ministers be removed five miles distant from the places of their usual supports and influences*. Such care is taken, and such is the advantage both of Law and Power, to strengthen the State, and restrain Dissenters. Nevertheless, the State *Ecclesiastical* hath advanced little in the esteem, acceptance, or acquiescence of people. The Dissenters are still the same, and are rather strengthned in their aversness. And those of them that repair to the publick Assemblies, retain their Principles of *Reformation* (as they speak) without seperation. The *Indifferent* sort of men are still indifferent, and it may be have some kindness for the depressed Party, and pity them in their Sufferings.

SECT.

SECT. XII.

The Extirpation of the Dissenters is both difficult and unprofitable.

PEradventure some think their total Extirpation to be the surest way to publick Security and Peace; and that great Severities will do the work. But Violent compulsion and Terror, comports not with the nature of Christian Religion, which is a *Rational Service*, and seeks a *willing people*; and is not at all in truth, where it is not received with *judgment* and *free choice*.

Besides, the success of such a course may be doubted of, since the Protestant spirit is not like the Popish, Cruel and outragious; and the nature of *English* men is not bloody, but generously compassionate. Wherefore in this Land to execute Extremity upon an intelligent, sober and peaceable sort of men, so numerous among all ranks, may prove exceeding difficult, unless it be executed by such Instruments as may strike terror into the whole Nation. The Civil Officers in general, may not be found so forward to afflict their quiet and harmless neighbours. Moreover, if severity used once for all, could extinguish an opposite party, there might be some plea of Policy; but when Severity must still be justified with more Severity, without an end, it is like to prove unlucky to the undertakers.

Nor is the Nation like to grow the better by the subversion of this sort, if it were effected. For in them no small part of the Nations Sobriety, Frugality, and Industry doth reside. They are not the *Great Wasters*, but mostly in the number of *Getters*. In most places the displaceing of them hath not encreased Civility and good Conversation among men; and it makes not for their dishonour, that many will swear and be drunk, to declare they are none of them.   E   There

There is something of more importance. To purge the
Nation of this people, may be to purge out more of its
Vitals, then the strength of this State can bear. To sup-
press those that are reckoned among the chief in Trading, and whose Commerce is so general, may beget a general diffidence and insecurity in Traders, and may help to
drive away Trade it self, and send it to an emulous and
encroaching Nation. May we mind, without offence, the
event of things among us? The business of the Nation
hath not proceeded with the current and free passage ex-
pected; nor doth its Wealth and Glory encrease. Trade
languisheth, and Traders fail in great Numbers; the Rents
of Lands fall; there is scarcity of Money in City and
Country; the Necessities and Difficulties of private E-
states are common, and Complainings are general. And
after a continued decay, things are at last fallen and
sunk much lower in the Ruins of the City of *LONDON*.
'Tis the Nations happiness to be re-established upon the
Ancient, Legal Foundations; but it is the right stating
and pursuing of its true Interest, by which it comes to a
firm consistency, and proportionable growth.

But this sort of men are inquisitive, and therefore trou-
blesome to Rulers, to whom Obedience without dispu-
ting, is most acceptable. It is fit indeed they be as humble
and modest, as inquisitive. Yet these inquiring men stand
much by that main Principle of *Protestantism*, the *Judgment of Discretion*. Indeed, the Churches Infallibility,
and the peoples implicite Faith, may help against all Disputes: but it cannot be so in *England*, whilst the people
read the Scriptures, and the established Doctrine of Faith
remains with us: And if no greater latitude can be allowed, then is at present, a Race of *Non-conformists* is like
to run parallel with the *Conformists* to the worlds end.

SECT.

SECT. XIII.

The representation of this Difficulty, is no Threatning to Rulers, or Intimation of Rebellion.

SUch as take this Representation for a Challenge to the Higher Powers, and a Demand of LIBERTY, and a Threatning, if it be not granted, are too far transported with Passion. What can be of greater concernment to Governors, then to discern and consider the state of their people, as it is indeed? And why may it not be minded by Subjects, and spoken of without any hint or thought of Rebellion? If Subjects use Arguments of Equity and Safety to Princes, it doth not presently speak a Demand: And it is no Threatning to say, *That Rulers themselves must be ruled by Reason, or do worse.*

The truth is, should they whose Case is here argued, upon this score meditate Rebellion and Warr, they were abandoned of their own Reason, and would hurry themselves into a precipice of manifest Ruin. To rush into ways of violence, evidently destroys their Interest, which stands in maintaining such works, and providing such things as are profitable to the Commonwealth, that it may be known that the publike good consists by them, as much as by others. To abide in their stations, to have patience under grievances, to sweeten their Governors by humility and modesty, is their best security, who stand or fall together with the true Interest of the Nation. Nevertheless, though a peoples discomposure doth not forespeak *Warrs* and *Tumults*, yet it may denounce *Woe* and *Misery*. Can nothing undo a Kingdom, but *Rebellion* and *Treason*? Was there ever a greater Separation from the Church of *England*, then now is? Was there ever less satisfaction among Multitudes every where, that

do

do yet frequent her Affemblies? A State, that is free
from violent Convulfive motions, may fall into a *Paraly-
tick*, or *Hectick* Diftemper, or an *Atrophy*. The Current
of Vital Blood may be ftopt in its Veins. There be ful-
len Mutinies, that make no noife, but may loofen all the
Joynts and Ligaments of Policy.

SECT. XIV.

The Setling of the Nation by an Eftablifhed Order, a Toleration, *and a* Connivence.

IF the Intereft both of Reformed Chriftianity, and of
this Kingdom, require a more comprehenfive ftate of
Religion, the true Extent of that State will be no impertinent or unmeet Inquiry. Such is the complicated condition
of Humane Affairs, that it is exceeding difficult to devife a
Rule or Model that fhall provide for all whom Equity
will plead for. Therefore the Prudent and Sober will
acquiefce in any Conftitution that is in fome good fort
proportionable to the Ends of Government. All that are
thought fit to abide with fecurity in any ftate, may be reduced to Three forts: Firft, Thofe that are of the Eftablifhed and Approved Order. 2. Such as may be Tole-
rated under certain Reftrictions. 3. Such as may be only connived at. And accordingly the Setling of a Nation may be made up of an *Eftablifhment*, a *Limited Toleration*, and a *Difcreet Connivence*. To be comprehended
within the *Eftablifhment*, it is requifite not only to be of
importance in the Publick Intereft, but alfo of Principles congruous to fuch ftated Order in the Church, as the
ftability of the Commonwealth requires. As for the two
later, *Toleration* and *Connivence*, they muft be regulated
with refpect not only to common Charity, but alfo to the
Safety of the Eftablifhed Order.

SECT

SECT. XV.

Of the Established Order in RELIGION, and the Moderation therein required.

AS for the *Established Order*, we presume not here to intermeddle with the Form or Species of Church-Government; but only to consider the prescribed Uniformity of Judgment and Practice. Evident reason speaks, That this be not narrow, but as broad and comprehensive as it is possible, that of it self, by its own force, it may be chief in sway, and controle all dissenting parties. On the other hand, it must not be loose and incoherent, but well compacted, that it may attain the Ends of Discipline, which are to promote sound Doctrine, and godly life, and to keep out Idolatry, Superstition, and all wicked Error and Practice that tends to the defeating of the Power of Christian Verity, Now these Ends do not require a Constitution of narrower bounds, then things necessary to Christian Faith and Life, and godly Order in the Church. These things must be maintained, and clearly stated; but whatsoever is more then these, may be matter of good intention and devotion to some, but an occasion of stumbling to others.

If it be said, *Who shall judg what things are necessary?* This doubt might soon be resolved, if passion, and prejudice, and private ends were vanquished. But however, let it be put to the Reason and Conscience of the Church of *England*: Why should not the great things of Christianity in the hands of wise Builders, be a sufficient Foundation of Church-Unity and Concord? What need hath the Church to enjoyn more then what is necessary to Faith and Order? Is not Moderation and Charity far more excellent, then glorying in Opinions, Formalities, and petty matters, to the regret of many Consciences? What if those that question

her

her Injunctions, should be weak, nice and captious? It is about matters of Divine Worship, wherein God hath proclaimed his Jealousie; and therefore if they being over-jealous, do erre, they deserve pity.

Our Ecclesiastical Superiors are here earnestly besought, Calmly and seriously to review the prescribed Uniformity, and to consider how some parts thereof, which at the best are but things indifferent, have been long disputed, and by what manner of men, and what hath been argued for and against them; and how this Difference hath held, and still encreased, from Bishop *Hooper* in King *Edward's* time, to the present *Non-conformists*; and then to judg whether a rational and conscientious man may not possibly dissent from some of these things, or at least doubt of their Lawfulness; and in case of such dissenting or doubting, what he should do, seeing the Apostle saith in the case of Meats, *He that doubts, is damned if he eat, because he eateth not of faith.* Can a man by Subscription and Practice, allow those things which his Conscience rationally doubts to be sinful?

It is Honour and Power enough for the Church, to be enabled by her Authority to inforce Gods Commandments. She is observed and honoured as a Mother indeed, when by her Wisdom and Care, her Children walk orderly according to the Christian Institution; and it may suffice her to chastise those of them that walk contrary to Christ. Though she be of *venerable Authority*; yet she doth not claim an *Infallibility*; and therefore she cannot settle the Conscience by her sole Warrant, but still leaves room for doubting. And in prescribed Forms and Rites of Religion, the Conscience that doth its office, will inevitably interpose and concern it self; and it being unsatisfied, jarrs and rents will follow. Woful Experience cryes unto us, *No more of such Injunctions then needs must.*

The

The indisputable Truths of Faith, and the indispensable. Duties of Life, are the main object of Church-Discipline; therefore an ill choice is made when the vigor of Discipline is exercised about lesser and more dispensable things of meer Humane Determination.

The Sons of the Church of *England* commend the Moderation used in the Articles of Religion, being formed in words of that extent, that men of different Perswasions about the Doctrines of *Predestination*, *Divine Grace*, and *Free-will*, did alike subscribe them. Nevertheless, the present *Orders* and *Ceremonies* inexorably imposed, have been as much disputed among the Godly Learned, as those different Opinions about the Doctrines aforesaid; and yet who can think they are of as much importance to the Substance of Religion?

Moreover, men might more easily agree in the use of these little things, or of some of them, were their Internal Judgments spared, and Subscriptions not injoyned. They may bear with others in the practice of some things, which themselves cannot practice. They may submit to some things, which they cannot approve; and that not for unworthy Ends, but for Conscience sake; and chuse rather to acquiesce in a *Tolerable State*, which for the main is found and good, rather then to endeavour a total Change, which may be mischievous, and at best is full of hazard. Wise men know, That by hasty Changes they do not come to rest and quietness, but only change their Old Grievances for New ones. If Practice sufficiently uniform, that is to say, without any scandalous difference, may be obtained from men of different Perswasions, Why should Uniformity of Judgment be exalted, and men tempted in doubtful points, to set their Consciences on the Rack? If any number of Dissenters were willing to do their uttermost towards Compliance, why should

need-

needless Choak-pears, which they could not swallow, be
forc'd upon them? If the Church's Authority be had in
reverence, if Order and Peace be kept, what matter is
it from what speculative Principles such observance pro-
ceeds? Though a man so complying, be not of the same
mind with his Superiors, yet he may have this honest
Catholick Principle, To promote the common Interest
of Reformed Christianity, and to dread the weakning
and shattering of it by needless Schisms. As for a narrow-
bounded Uniformity both in Opinions, and petty Obser-
vations, it is no more necessary in the Church, then Uniformity of Complexions and Visages in the same Civil
State; and is indeed no more attainable, where a generous Freedom of Judgment is allowed.

SECT. XVI.

*Whether the Dissenters are capable of being brought into
such a Comprehension.*

WHilst Reason is urged on their behalf that are
left without the lines of the present Establishment, some haply may ask, *Will they themselves hearken to
reason?* Be it supposed that some among them seem not re-
ducible to a due publick Order; but another sort there
are, and those of chiefest moment, whose principles are
fit for Government; the stability whereof hath been ex-
perimented in those Countreys where they have had the
effectual concurrence of the Civil Powers. Their Way
never yet obtained in *England*, nor were they ever fa-
voured with the Magistrates vigorous aid, so much as for
an Accommodation with the Established Polity: But
their difficulties have still encreased; and how streight so-
ever the Terms imposed on them, were in times before, the
after-times have still made them streighter. Wherefore

it

if they have been too much addicted to their own Opinions, or have committed some errors in the management of
their Affairs, it is no marvel. It was not easie for them,
being destitute of the Magistrates influence, and lying under great discouragement and disadvantage, always to keep
stable and sure footing in such a slippery place as Church-
Discipline. The asserting of their Discipline, is not here
intended; but the Inquiry is, *Whether they be of a Judgment
and Temper that makes them capable of being brought under
the Magistrates Paternal Care and Conduct, to such a stated
Order as will comport with this Church and Kingdom?*

This is no undertaking Discourse, it presumes only to
offer its Reason to equal and impartial *Readers*. When a
Divine of great fame, and of much esteem with the chiefest of the *English* Clergy, was taxed by the Jesuit his Ad-
versary, for being no *Protestant*, as refusing to subscribe
the Nine and thirty Articles; he judged it a sufficient An-
swer to testifie his belief, *That the Doctrine of this Church
was so pure and holy, that whosoever lived according to it,
should undoubtedly be saved; & that there was nothing in it that
might give just cause to any to forsake the Communion, or disturb
the Peace thereof.* Who, or what is there almost, that this
or the like Latitude would not encompass, when hearty
endeavours are put forth to gain men? The same Catholick Spirit may dwell both in larger and stricter judgments. One that cannot subscribe to all things contained in a Volume of Doctrines and Rules compiled by men
subject to error, may be ready to joyn with any Church
not depraved in the substance of Religion, that doth not
impose upon his belief or practice, things unsound or doubtful, as the terms of her Communion.

The *Presbyterians* generally hold the *Church of England*
to be a true Church, though defective in its Order and
Discipline; and frequent the Worship of God in the pub-
F   like

like Aſſemblies. And many of thoſe that preſs earneſtly after further Reformation, do yet communicate as well in the Sacraments, as the Word Preached, and Prayer. And a way might be opened for many more to do as much, by a ſafe and eaſie condeſcention of thoſe in Authority.

The Miniſters of the *Presbyterian* Perſwaſion, in their Propoſals preſented to His Majeſty, declare, That they do not, nor ever did renounce the true Ancient Primitive *Epiſcopacy*, or Preſidency, as it was ballanced or managed by a due commixtion of *Presbyters* therewith. That they are ſatisfied in their judgments concerning the Lawfulneſs of a Liturgy or Form of Worſhip; and they Petition His Majeſty, That for the ſetling of the Church in Unity and Peace, ſome Learned, Godly, and Moderate Divines, indifferently choſen, may be employed to compile a Form, as much as may be, in Scripture-words; or at leaſt to Reviſe, and effectually Reform the Old. Concerning Ceremonies, they profeſs to hold themſelves obliged in every part of Divine Worſhip, to do all things decently and in order; and to be willing therein to be determined by Authority, in ſuch things as being meerly circumſtantial, are common to humane actions, and are to be ordered by the Light of Nature, and Humane Prudence, according to the general Rules of Gods Word. But as for divers Ceremonies formerly retained in the Church of *England*, in as much as they contribute nothing to the neceſſary decency which the Apoſtle required, and draw too near the ſignificancy and moral efficacy of Sacraments, and have been rejected together with Popery, by many of the Reformed Churches abroad, and ever ſince the Reformation, have been matter of endleſs Diſpute in this Church, and an occaſion of great ſeperation, and are at the beſt, indifferent, and in their own nature mutable, they deſire they be not impoſed; and they heartily acknowledg his Majeſty

sty to be Supreme Governour over all Persons, and over all Things and Causes in these his Dominions.

Upon these Proposals, His Majesty in His Declaration concerning Ecclesiastical Affairs, hath thus graciously expressed himself: "We must for the Honour of all those of "either Perswasion, with whom We have conferred, de-"clare, That the Professions and Desires for the advance-"ment of true Piety and Godliness, are the same; their "professions of Zeal for the Peace of the Church, the "same; of Affection and Duty to Us, the same. They all "approve Episcopacy; they all approve a set-form of Li-"turgy; and they all disapprove and dislike the sin of Sa-"criledg and Alienation of the Revenues of the Church. "And if upon these Excellent Foundations, in submission "to which there is such a harmony of Affections, any Su-"perstructure should be raised to the shaking of these "Foundations, or the contracting and lessening of the "blessed gift of Charity, which is a vital part of Chri-"stian Religion, We shall think our selves very unfortu-"nate, and even suspect that We are defective in that Ad-"ministration of Goverument with which God hath intrust-"ed Us.

After these things, the Ministers commissioned for the Review of the Liturgy, in their account of that Business, thus address themselves to His Majesty: "Though the "Reverend Bishops have not had time to consider of our "Additions to the Liturgy, and of our Reply; We hum-"bly crave that it may be considered before a Determi-"nation be made. Though we seem to have laboured in "vain, we shall lay this Work of Reconciliation at Your "Majesties feet. We must believe, that when Your Ma-"jesty took our Consent to a Liturgy to be a Foundati-"on, that would infer our Concord; You meant not, that "we should have no Concord, but by consenting to this

Litur-

"Liturgy without any confiderable Alterations. And
" when Your Majefty commanded us by Letters Patents,
" to meet about fuch Alterations as were needful, or expe-
" dient to give fatisfaction to tender Confciences, and
" the reftoring and continuing of Peace and Unity; We
" reft affured it was not Your Majefties fenfe that thofe
" tender Confciences fhould be forced to practice all which
" they judg unlawful, or not fo much as a Ceremony
" fhould be abated them; or that our Treaty was only
" to convert either party to the Opinion of another; and
" that all our hopes of Liberty and Concord, confifted
" only in difputing the Bifhops into *Non-conformity*, or
" coming in every Ceremony to their mind.

This is the Church's mifery, That when any particular
Intereft grows in Profperity and Power, and can carry all
before it, Condefcention prefently ceafeth on that fide.
And fo the difagreeing parties in the feveral viciffitudes of
Publick Affairs, tread down one another, and juftifie
themfelves by the like mifcarriages of their Oppofites
when time was. By this means the Church's diftempers
and breaches are perpetuated, and Religion in general fuffers
much damage and fcorn. But it would be the glory of that
party that ftands on the Vantage-ground, to give a lead-
ing Example of unconftrained Moderation.

SECT. XVII.

*Acquiefcence in the Widened Eftablifhment, is the Safety of
Religion.*

IF it be faid, That a little yeelding doth but make way
for further Incroachments; we fuppofe that Governors know how far to truft, and what it is fit to grant,
if fubjects know not what is fit for them to ask. Perfons
allowed in the Publick Service, may eafily be kept in
that

that dependance on the State, which shall prevent the danger of an *Anti-Clergy.* We suppose likewise, that a sound Church-Government is not so weak and tottering, that the Abatement of some Rigors in things at best but indifferent, will hazard its overturning.

The wiser sort of Dissenters, whose Conformity, were they gained, would most avail, are weary of these strifes, and consider what is passable in the state of *England,* and might settle this Church. They dread the Consequents of Changes, the hurrying into other Extreams, and the wild excursions of some spirits. They would not be left again to the late uncertainty, and continual Vacillations in Government; and they have long since seen the manifold Errors committed in the Policy of the late times. They know that such unfixed Liberty would not secure them. And therefore it may well be thought, they would accept reasonable terms, and rest satisfied therein.

But this Consideration is taken by the wrong Handle, if this sober and steddy part of the *Non-conformists* be slighted and judged the less considerable, because they are cast into one condition as to the Law, with others that are of more unmanageable and unstable Principles. For who can tell how time may work out things, and frame the Spirits of the unsober to a greater soberness, and dispose them to a better consistency among themselves? But howsoever, can it make for the Publick Weal, That the more discreet and moderate sort, that might easily be brought in, should be inforced to continue the chief reputation and strength of a divided Party?

SECT. XVIII.

Of Toleration *and* Connivence.

LET Impartial Reason judg, Whether a swaying, or at least a momentous part of those that close not with the present state Ecclesiastical, may not be incompassed in an Establishment of such a latitude, as may happily settle this Church, and consequently promote the Peace, Wealth and Honour of the Civil State.

As for others that are of sound Belief, and good Life, yet have taken in some Principles of Church-Government less congruous to National Settlement, I would never be a means of exposing them to Oppression, Contempt and Hatred, but would admit their Plea, as far as it will go. For if God hath received them, why should their fellow-servants reject or afflict them causlesly? Every true Christian should be tender of all that love the Lord Jesus in sincerity.

Nevertheless, their Liberty pleaded for, is not to be inordinate, but measured and limited by the safety of true Religion in general, and of the publick Established Order; which is not unpracticable: For the world wants not an Experiment of the safety of a Toleration or Indulgence so regulated.

SECT. XIX.

Dissenters of Narrow and Rigid Principles, advised to Moderation.

AS Authority may be too prone to err in the Severity of Imposing; so Subjects may be too wilful in refusing to obey. As an explicit Assent, and Approbation, may by Superiors be too rigidly exacted in doubtful

things;

things; so the unreasonable stiffness and harshness of Inferiors, may keep them from that compliance in practice, which their Conscience (becalm'd from Passion and Prejudice) would not gainsay. A servile, fawning, temporizing Spirit, is vile enough; but that which is sedate, castigate, and subdued to Reason, is not only pleasing to Governours, but also of great avail for Publick Peace.

Every Christian should be deeply sensible of the common Interest of Reformed Christianity, which is incomparably more valuable then those private Opinions, and little narrow Models, which may have much of his fancy and affection. Well-minded persons may easily be deceived touching their private Sentiments in Religion. They may think they are under the uncontrolable Sway of Conscience, when indeed they are but bound up by Custom, Education, Complexion, or some other kind of Prejudice. For ones own sake, one would gladly be rid of such Confinements, and walk more at liberty: But much more should one strive to be as comprehensive as may be, for the common safety, and advancement of true Religion, which cannot stand by such uncertainty and multiplicity of petty forms, but requires an ample and well-setled state, to defend and propagate it against the amplitude and potency of the *Romish* Interest. The prudent and sober should not easily settle upon such Opinions in Church-Order, as will never settle the Nation, but tend rather to infinite perplexity and discomposure.

Howsoever, I will not bear too hard upon any thing that may fairly pretend to Conscience, which, though erroneous, should not be harshly dealt with. Nevertheless, if (when all is said) some dissatisfaction doth invincibly possess the Judgment, in that case Christian Humility and Charity, as well as Discretion, adviseth such persons to acquiesce in their private Security and Freedom, and not

to

to reach after that Liberty that may unsettle the Publick Order, and undermine the Common Safety.

SECT. XX.

This Comprehensive State of Religion further considered, with respect to Three important Interests: First to that of the KING.

FOR the removing of all conceived Prejudices, let this desired Latitude of Religion, be considered with respect to the several Interests of the King, of the Church and Clergy, and of the Nobility and Gentry. First let it be examined in reference to the Interest of Regal Majesty.

The *Non-conformists*, and others inclinable to their way, are by some charged with such Principles as detract much from Kingly Power and Dignity, and tend to advance Popular Faction. It is confessed, they have been eager Assertors of Legal Liberties ; yet herein they were not singular, but in almost all PARLIAMENTS have had the concurrence of many good Patriots that were not touch'd with the least tincture of *Puritanism*. They profess much affection to MONARCHY, and the Royal Family; and think they have made it appear by their hazardous declaring against the designed Death of our late Soveraign, and their vigorous Actings for the Restitution of His Majesty that now is. They are so well satisfied, as none more, in the Ancient Fundamental Constitution of this Kingdom.

This Arraignment of their supposed Principles about Government, may haply proceed upon Mistake. There is reason enough to think, That the many late Disputes about Prerogative and Liberty, are *Controversiæ ortæ non primæ*, that they had their rise from something else, which lyes at the bottom. Both former and present times
do

do shew, That the *Anti-Puritan* Interest, when occasion serves, and the urgency of Affairs requires, can contest with Princes, and pretend Conscience too, in crossing their Designs. Inclinations and Interests, more then Speculative Opinions, will be found to have born the sway, and caused those active motions on the one hand, and the other. These *Dogmata* or Problemes about Obedience and Government, do but little, where mens Affections and Concernments do not give them spirit and vigor. The practical Judgment of Inferiors, hath a bias in this case, according to their Superiors Benignity or Asperity towards them. High strains of speech may easily proceed from such as flatter their Governors, or know not themselves; but they are worthy of credit, that speak credible things.

The wise man saith, *He that repeateth a matter, separateth very friends.* A looking back to former discords, marrs the most hopeful Redintegration. Acts of Indempnity, are Acts of Oblivion also, and must be so observed. Let not the way of Peace be barr'd by the framing of such Tests as may perplex the minds of men, but add no real security to the Higher Powers. For as some set their wits a work in framing, so do others in evading the designs of such Engagements. And of those that devise how to evade them, some may deal seriously, and others perhaps may trifle with Conscience; but the internal Judgments of both remain what they were before. The common Evasions or Violations of such bonds among all parties in our times, do shew, That they are not the way to root out inveterate Opinions. But there is a surer way to obviate the evil tendency of such Opinions, and to render them ineffectual. For it is not this or that narrow conception or notion, but some greater thing, that rules the actions of humane life. The condition of the dissatisfied, may without damage, or just scandal to any, be made such, That their far greater

G num-

number shall not long for changes, but gladly embrace present things; and then the implacably evil-minded would want matter to work upon, and rest without hope of disturbing the Publick Peace.

Moreover, all Loyal Principles are not inclosed in some Positions, in which may be much variety and uncertainty of opinion, and in which both Theological and Political Casuists (and they great Assertors of Monarchical Government) have written doubtfully. Men of different apprehensions in such things, may be indued with the same prudence, soberness, common charity, love of Publick Tranquility, reverence of Regal Majesty, conscience of Allegiance, and an awful regard of Divine and Humane Laws. Men of nicer Judgments, may have as loyal hearts as those of greater latitude. And why should the judgments of such men be rack'd, and their spirits vexed with curious scrutinies? The ancient Sacred Bonds of Fidelity, are not questioned; and if they do not, what others can oblige and awe the Conscience?

The extent of Prerogatives Royal, of the Priviledges of PARLIAMENTS, and of the Peoples Immunities, is not matter fit for common disquisition, but requires to be kept among the Secrets of Government. It might have been far better, if these points had been more gently and warily handled on all sides. The *English* (in general) are an ingenuous and open-hearted people; and if unlucky accidents discompose them not, they are of themselves disposed to have their Kings in great veneration; and doubtless their satisfaction and good estate, is their Soveraigns true repose.

SECT. XXI.

Secondly, *To the Interest of the Church and Clergy.*

IN the next place, let this Comprehensive state be examined, with respect to the Interest of the *Church of England.* The Doctrine of Faith and Sacraments by Law established, is heartily received by the *Non-conformists*, and it is like to be the Basis of their standing in *England*, as long as Protestant Religion stands. How far they approve *Episcopacy* and *Liturgy*, hath been above declared. Their dissent is in some parts of Divine Worship (as they say) not appointed of God, but devised by men; also in the frame of the *English Hierarchy*, as it differs from the Ancient Episcopacy; and they avow they are under no obligation to extirpate or impeach that ancient Form. The Ministers of this Perswasion are Godly and Learned, able and apt to teach the people; and no small part of the Congregations in *England* feel the loss of them. Doth the Lord of the Harvest command that such Labourers be thrust out of his Service? And will the chief Shepherd at his appearing justifie this usage of his faithful Servants?

The Bishops and dignified Clergy, and those of their Perswasion, have the advantage of Law and Power. But can they believe that the Church of God in these Nations, is terminated in them alone? It is hoped that Christ hath a larger Interest in these Realms. Shall it be said of the *English Prelacy*, That it cannot stand without the ejection of Thousands of Orthodox, Pious Ministers? Or that it dreads a general diffusion of knowledg in the people? Or that this is a Maxime thereof, *No Ceremony, no Bishop*; as if the Bishop's work were at an end, and his office of no force, if Ceremonies were left indifferent? Is an Ecclesiastical Government, that pleads Apostolical Instituti-

on,

on, and Universal reception, so weak and feeble, that godly and peaceable men, preaching only the indubitable truths of Christianity, would undermine it? If any should preach what is Schismatical and Seditious, they are liable to Restraints and Censures, according to their demerits. Why will the established Clergy refuse their Brethren, and set them at such a distance? Is it their honour, strength, or safety, that such men should be numbred among their opposites?

The intrinsick and permanent State of *Prelacy*, is not advanced by these present Rigors. It is not more rooted in the hearts of people, nor are many gained over that would stick close to it in a time of tryal. The dread, that is of its Censures, ariseth from the subsequent temporal Penalties. And however it be, its Chariot drives but heavily. It cannot measure its strength by the number of *Conformists*, among whom there are many that are a reproach unto it, and many that are very indifferent men; and there are the *Latitudinarians*, that are accounted but luke-warm *Conformists*; and many that submit, may not like the imposing; and men may think divers Injunctions (that are not simply unlawful) to be burdensome and inconvenient, and would be glad to shake off the yoke. A great Prelate before the late Warrs, is reported to say, *That the Conforming Puritan was the Devil of the Times.* And of those that zealously affect the established Order, there are not a few that disgust the behaviour of Church-men, and are ready to upbraid them with the known moderation of many whom they have ejected; yea, the more considerate Sons of the Church, do observe and bewail such dangerous miscarriages by *Simony, Pluralities, Non-residency*, and *Profaneness*, as threaten a second downfall. The world takes notice what men are cast out; and what is the condition of multitudes that are retained in the Service of the Church.

There

There are a sort of men of great Worth and Reputation
in the several Orders of this Kingdom, that indeed affect
Episcopacy, but see the inconvenience and danger of this
Severity, and would have things carried with Discretion
and Equity, and are ready to do good offices for the depressed Party. If the Affairs of the Commonwealth should go
backwards, can the Clergy alone be at rest in their Honour,
Power and Wealth? Though of later times it hath been said,
No Bishop, no King ; yet it is not evident, That the present
frame of Prelacy hath an immutable Interest in the Regal
Name and Power.

The Religion of any State will sink, if it be not held up
in its venerable Estimation among the people ; and it cannot be long held in reverence, if it hath neither the reality,
nor appearance of Devotion and Sanctity. That which is
divested of the Disguises and Impostures of *Romish* Superstition, had need to be spirited with Life and Power. Minds
touch'd with Devotion, will look either to the way of true
and real Godliness, or to the Popish Bodily Exercise. It is
here sincerely wish't, That the Clergy may hold their state
in safety and honour ; That they may never be laid low for
want of meet Revenue or Dignity ; That they may always
preserve a reverend esteem of their Persons and Office. But
then the Bishops must not be the Head of such Ministers, as
for ignorance and lewdness are a scandal and scorn to their
Neighbours ; nor of such as incourage profaneness, and de-
prave seriousness and diligence in Religion and strictness of
life, under the scandal of *Puritanism, Fanaticism* , or such
like names of reproach. They must so manage their Government, that under it the sound knowledg of God may
encrease through the Land ; that holiness and righteousness
may flourish ; that their influence may dispose men to do
those things that are honest, and pure, and comely, and ver-
tuous, and praise-worthy. To this may be added the setling

of

of the Church in a due extent, that it may incompass so much as may enable it to vanquish whatsoever is inconsistent with it; and to keep within compass whatsoever may be tollerated under it.

The great danger and damage which may be dreaded to ensue this moderation, (which nevertheless may possibly not ensue it) is but the cutting off some Luxuriances from some in the Highest Order; or the sharing among many what was ingrossed by a few. And the Church doth not change for the worse, if some diminution of greatness in a very few persons makes way for a more general amplitude, stability and peace; and the Clergy enjoy an Estate of Power, Plenty and Honour, with less envy and hazard of undermining.

SECT. XXII.

Thirdly, *To the Interest of the Nobility and Gentry.*

THere is another Interest, that of the *Nobility* and *Gentry*, which is worthy of regard in this Inquiry. The Latitude and Liberty here discoursed, is thought to give too great advantage to the *Citizens* and the *Commonalty*; as also to make all sorts more knowing, and less servile; and consequently, less obsequious to the wills of great men. And the doubt is, whether the Nobles and Gentlemen of *England* can maintain their Authority and Splendor, with the Freedom of Citizens and the common people. Surely in the times of their Ancestors they were in as much splendor and power, as they have been in the memory of this Age; and yet in those times both Citizens and Yeomanry were rich and free, brave and worthy in their own rank. And it may be the higher Degrees in *England* would never be so advanced, as some have conceited, if the meaner sort were reduced to the condition of the *French* Peasantry. For there is another Spirit in the *English* People, which peradventure

may

may not be vanquished at less charges then dissipation of
the strength and riches, an l all the glory of this Land, Besides, Trade which is the Life of *England*, must be managed
by a people not of a slavish and sordid condition. And in
a Trading Nation, things do so pass to and fro, and run from
one hand to another, that New Men by their Wealth will
be always getting up into the rank of Gentlemen, and former Gentile Families will be decaying. There is a Liberty
for every Native to purchase Lands ; and though some of
our Tenures began in the Vassalage of meaner men to great
ones, yet they are now by custom of later Ages, become so
far free, that they are fit for any ingenuous persons to take
them up. Moreover, the *English* Gentry are Commons, according to the main frame of this Polity ; and that great
Convention where they meet in their chiefest Power, is the
Commons House of Parliament, in which they represent the
universality of the Commons of all Counties, and Cities,
and Burroughs: And therefore the free Estate of the Commons, is the true Interest of Gentlemen. And how ground-
less and fruitless is all evil emulation between the Gentry
and Citizens, or Traders! For they mutually uphold each
other, or both must fall to the ground. Many Gentile Families are the Off-spring of former Citizens ; and many Citizens are the sons of Gentlemen. And when the Estates of
ancient Gentry are sinking, their Marriage with Citizens is
an ordinary means of underpropping them. And if Traders fail, the Revenue of the Gentry must fail also ; whose
Lands did never bear that Price, nor yeeld that Annual
Rent that of late they have done, till the Nation became
great in Foreign Trade. If emulation of Gallantry be any
matter of grudg between them, the Citizens may leave the
Gentry to their own Garbs, and retain a grave habit to
themselves, in which they may sufficiently express their
Wealth, as their Predecessors did before them. For it is

generous so to do. And as for the Nobility and Gentry, their Honour lyes in upholding their Families, and bearing sway in their Countries; and they do the one by discreet and liberal Frugality; and the other by having and using greater Abilities then the vulgar, for their Countries Service.

SECT. XXIII.

The general Security that comes by this Latitude.

THE chief Prejudices have been considered; and these three Important Interests being known aright are found not to oppose, but to require this Latitude of Religion. Furthermore, our common Security and Freedom, earnestly perswades it: For the Severities of Law against Dissenters, may at length come home to them or theirs, who take themselves to be far out of the reach thereof. And the inforcing of those Penalties may need such ways and means, as may trouble them who are tender of the Lawful Rights and Liberties of *English*-men. But the Common Peace being once firmly setled in this Comprehensive state, all Necessity of Powers and Proceedings extraordinary, will disappear, and vanish away.

Finally, The more Pacifick we are at home, the more Powerful and Formidable shall we be abroad. But our Breaches are too well known, and make little for our Reputation or Advantage in Foreign parts. What can it avail, to disturb a People that would settle in peace, and whose Peace is accommodated to the Publick Weal, and bound up together with it? It must needs be fruitless and unfortunate, and cause perplexities and miscarriages in the chiefest Affairs of State. It is a saying of the wisest of Kings, *He that troubles his own House, shall inherit the wind.*

FINIS.

www.ingramcontent.com/pod-product-compliance
Lightning Source LLC
Chambersburg PA
CBHW022036080426
42733CB00007B/853